D0712920

Gramma Darling

By Lissa Schroeder

Illustrated by Doron Ben-Ami

Outskirts Press, Inc.
http://www.outskirtspress.com

DENVER, COLORADO

Paperback ISBN: 978-1-4327-8402-7
Hardback ISBN: 978-1-4787-5790-0

Library of Congress Control Number: 2015912490

Outskirts Press and the "OP" logo are trademarks belonging to Outskirts Press, Inc.

PRINTED IN THE UNITED STATES OF AMERICA

Gramma Darling

Dedicated to Dorothy Raines
The authentic, deeply loved Gramma Darling.
Thank you for all the time and love you gave this little girl
and for always believing in me.

Lissa

I dedicate this to my mother,
known by her grandchildren as "GrammaRita."
and cherished for the love and wisdom she has shared through the years.

Doron

By Lissa Schroeder
Illustrated by Doron Ben-Ami

It is truly extraordinary, the difference one woman can make in the life of a child. For me, it was my grandmother — one of my very favorite people in the whole world. Gramma loved kids, and she liked having us around when we were growing up. We spent lots of weekends with her, and whole weeks at a time in the summers. She lived in a little Minnesota town called Quamba (kwahm'buh), population 123.

And she was the most beautiful, wonderful woman that ever was.

When one of us grandkids would be just learning to walk, Gramma would hold out her arms and say, "Come to Gramma, darling, come to Gramma!" That's how Grandma Dorothy became Gramma Darling. The nickname stuck, you see, because it fit her so well. She was the dearest, twinkliest lady. And Gramma always laughed. She was great for laughing. But mostly, she just loved us.

Gramma always moved fast. Full of energy, she never seemed to be still, but was always busy doing something or other. She used to say she couldn't even get a tan when she mowed the lawn, because the sun couldn't catch her. Maybe it had something to do with her being a waitress at the Sportsmen's Café for over 50 years!

Her favorite part of the job was talking and laughing with all the old friends and customers she'd known for ages . . . some of them for three or four generations.

We would visit her there at work, very early in the morning, sitting on swivel seats at the counter, eating cottage cheese and pears with paprika. She would give us each quarters for the juke box and let us choose our own songs while she zoomed this way and back, and that way, and this way again, taking orders and bringing food to all the people sitting at the tables. She only stopped long enough to tell everyone in the place that we were her grandkids. She was very proud of us.

There were so many fascinating things to explore at Gramma's house. To us, it was a wonderland of open romping grounds, with mysterious nooks full of discoveries to make, inside and out.

Her house sat on its own little hill surrounded by hedges. Upstairs, pretty curtains hung in the gable windows that stood out of the sloping roof. Leading from the road up to the front porch, a cement sidewalk climbed the hill in seven steps. At the top stood a black steel lamppost with Gramma's address hanging on a plaque beneath, swinging from its curlicue arm. We used to sled down that hill in the winter; and if we were feeling very brave, ride our bikes down its steep, grassy slope in the summer.

A huge elm tree dwarfed the house, standing with branches spreading to the sky. It dominated the side yard. How we loved that tree! It took three of us holding hands to reach all the way around it. One of its wide lower limbs had a swoop in it shaped like a saddle. I used to sit up there for hours, reading and swinging my feet, or eating fresh rhubarb dipped in sugar, or just daydreaming while the wind whispered and sighed through the leaves above me.

Flowers grew all around Gramma's house. By the side porch near the water spigot was a big patch of hanging bluebells, and in the corner was a riot of orange tiger lilies pouncing in the breeze. They were almost as tall as I was. All along the driveway on both sides were lofty lilac bushes blooming all purply sweet, casting their thick fragrance across the yard and attracting fat, fuzzy, brown and yellow bumblebees.

She also had a vegetable garden. We used to help her water and weed it. Weeding in the sun was hot work, and it was itchy. We got all sweaty, and the gnats stuck to our faces. When we tried to wipe them away we'd smear mud all over, too. But there was just something primevally satisfying about getting our hands in the dirt and taming growing things; to smell the damp earth and feel the tightly grasping roots pull free, to look behind us and see the straight, green rows of corn and peas, beans, potatoes, and tomato plants standing unrivaled in the rich brown soil.

Sometimes it was tricky, though, to tell which plants were weeds and which were not. Weeds were sneaky. One kind looked just like a baby corn plant, and another looked like a ferny carrot top. Sometimes we pulled up a good plant by accident, but Gramma Darling never got mad.

Behind the house, a path led to Grampa's old workshop. Inside, everything was still and dry and smelled a little musty. There was only one small window, so even in daylight everything was in shadow. To us, it was a hallowed place, full of sacred silence. We stepped softly and whispered when we went in there. It felt so empty without him.

On the workbench along one side were a myriad of neglected hand tools and coffee cans full of nuts and bolts. Up the ladder, in the loft, were trunks full of lonely old dolls, a baby cradle shrouded in dust, an ancient metal highchair, a faded red rocking horse sagging sadly on his rusted springs, and heaps of other discarded toys and furniture we'd worn out or long outgrown.

Leaning against the wall, dreaming of winter, was a glorious six-foot toboggan that five of us could ride at a time. Made of sturdy wood, it had thick, twisted rope handles all down the sides, and the front curled up like a sleigh. It reigned undisputed as King of the Snow, but for now, could only stand and wait patiently for its season to return.

We never stayed long in that lonesome place, but after a little while of softly exploring, with relief, we would head back out into the sunshiny, flowery, run-through-the-grass world.

Outside, in the trees, we found robins' nests full of bald baby birds, chirping and weaving and stretching upward hungrily. Being careful not to touch them, we dropped caterpillars and insects into their wide-open mouths.

If we sat very still near the pond, beautiful dragonflies would land on us, all shimmery bright blue or purple, fanning their iridescent wings. With their multifaceted eyes, like glimmering green golf balls, they kept a sharp watch for passing mosquito snacks, and soon zipped away.

But it was hard to sit still for long, with the big wide world inviting us to discover exciting new things; so off we went, laughing and tripping over each other, chasing slippery, spotted leopard frogs through the tall grass. We collected bright, neon-green tree frogs with bulging red eyes and round orange toes that we found clinging to the screen doors. We caught brown baby toads, no bigger than marbles. They were funny—so clumsy and wrinkly and bumpy, that they'd flip themselves over trying to hop away. Sometimes we brought home butterflies or garter snakes or painted mud turtles, or the fat, sleepy, black salamanders with big yellow spots that we found in the window wells.

Gramma didn't mind. She would help us make homes for them in shoe boxes or ice-cream buckets, so we could gently play with them for a while. Come twilight we'd let them all go, and we would chase fireflies through the fields, like running through an ocean of stars . . . catching them in mayonnaise jars with holes punched in the lids. Gramma would set the jars of brightly flashing beetles on our dresser like tiny, blinking night-lights.

Usually we would spend the whole day outside, only popping in to grab a quick peanut butter sandwich or an apple, but on rainy days we played indoors.

Our favorite room was the big, closed-in front porch. It was long and narrow, running the width of the house, with lots of windows on three sides, and the front company door. In it were tall dollhouses full of curious things, toy cars with whole cities to drive them through, a pile of stuffed animals we could bury ourselves in, and shelves full of books and games.

One end of the porch was stacked with brightly colored fabrics next to Gramma's sewing machine. There, with her old black Pfaff humming away, she made the loveliest, toasty-warm quilts in square and pointy patterns and curving shapes of every design. She also made clothes for all the baby dolls and teddy bears.

On stormy days it seemed exhilaratingly dangerous to be in there, with the rain slashing down all around us, while lightning split the angry sky, and slamming thunder shook the house and rolled away in deep, rumbling echoes. It tried to make us feel very small and frightened; but Gramma Darling was near, and it was comforting to know that the howling storm couldn't get at us, no matter how hard it crashed and whined and rattled the windows.

A long, narrow stairway climbed to the bedrooms above. We always skipped the fifth step because if we put our weight on it, it creaked out a low, ghostly ggrrooooooan. The stairs ended at a circular landing with four doors. We used to play up there with all the doors closed so it felt like a secret indoor tree house.

Behind those doors were the Gold Room, the Red Room, the Blue Room, and Gramma's Room. The Gold Room was big; bright and sunny with two gable windows standing out over the roof. Everything was decorated in rich tones of yellows and golds.

The Red Room was smaller and darker, with only one window closely shaded by a maple tree right outside. It had rose-colored walls, a hard wooden floor with two slippery red rugs, and a lacy bedspread of deep red, with long, silky tassels that hung to the floor. The closet had no door. It was the only room we were afraid to sleep in. There was just something spooky about that open closet at night. It played tricks on our imaginations, especially while tree branches were tapping and scratching against the windowpane.

The Blue Room was for the kids; a cheerful place with walls of baby blue. A fancy dresser stood on four feet shaped like lions' paws and was so tall we couldn't see the top of it or look in any of the highest drawers. Whoever slept on the inside of the bed had to watch out not to whack their head on the slanted ceiling. The crib was for the babies. There were lots of babies. Gramma had 15 of us grandkids.

Everyone loved to linger in Gramma's kitchen. It smelled of every good thing. She was a marvelous cook. For breakfast she would make us chocolate chip peanut butter banana pancakes or steamy waffles with blueberry syrup. Dinner might be the juiciest, crispiest, salty fried chicken with just-picked corn on the cob and mashed potatoes & gravy, or her fabulous homemade chicken and rice soup with thick slices of bread and butter.

All summer she had fresh garden veggies on the table, too. She cut cartwheel cucumber slices, oh-so-good pale green kohlrabi wedges, crunchy carrot sticks, and snap-crackly red radishes, all bobbing in fancy glass dishes of ice water, to be eaten with a sprinkling of salt. They were almost as good as dessert . . . almost.

Gramma Darling was famous for her desserts. She would make four kinds of pie at a time, or her secret recipe for the gooiest chocolaty cherry cake with whole cherries inside. And there were always cookies, some shaped like peanuts and some like maple leaves.

But it wasn't the adventures or the exploring or the dozens of fun places to play that we loved most about Gramma's house. The very best thing . . . was Gramma Darling. She was always busy, but never too busy to spend time with us. She didn't mind kids swarming all around her or asking lots of questions.

We helped her wrap the coins from her waitressing tips, we helped her stir the soup, we helped her with the grocery shopping, and she let us choose which flavor of ice cream to buy. She let us roll out the cookie dough with the floury rolling pin, stamp out gingerbread men with the heavy metal cutter, and decorate them with raisins and licorice whips and Red Hots for eyes. Then we would wait with all our might while they baked, filling the house with the aroma of piping-hot, cinnamon-gingery goodness.

In the evening, when it got dark, she would do jigsaw puzzles with us at the kitchen table, or play cards, or teach the girls how to thread a needle and sew a button back on Teddy Bear's pajamas.

Sometimes we would write funny skits. Gramma would sit and be our audience while we acted them out for her. She would laugh and laugh. She was such a great one for laughing.

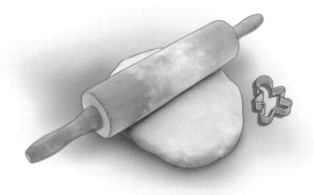

At night she would run warm bubble baths with extra bubbles to wash off all the good clean dirt we'd accumulated on those perfect, blissful days. It was okay to bring several nice toys into the tub, and she understood that a reasonable amount of splashing was necessary for a really thorough wash. We never came out until the water was so cold our teeth were chattering. She'd wrap us up in fluffy warm towels and gently comb out the girls' tangles.

Once we were in our jammies, she would take turns holding us tightly cheek-to-cheek and dancing all around the living room to the music on the radio, even when we grew so big our feet hung almost to her knees.

When it got late we would curl up in her lap, all heavy-eyed, as she softly smoothed our hair and read a book. Then she would carry the youngest one up to bed and tuck us in, all snug and cozy under the quilts she made with her own busy hands, and we would tumble into happy dreams, knowing we were precious to her and very much loved.

Looking back, I realize what a rare and priceless gift I was given, to have received so much of her time and attention. Gramma didn't have to buy us expensive gifts or take us on exotic vacations; she was just *there* with us. Somehow she understood the impact we can all make, and the enduring connections we can create, by spending simple quality time with the little ones in our lives. Childhood is so fleeting.

Just by sharing herself with me, and including me in the small events of her daily life, she was creating the happiest memories of my childhood. Her home was a magical place for me, a refuge of calm and peace where I felt safe and significant and loved.

It is truly extraordinary, the difference one woman can make in the life of a child.

I'm all grown up now and have three children of my own; each, in turn, toddling to Gramma's outstretched arms. Following her example, I've tried to raise them with as much consideration and care as I received from that one remarkable woman . . . and do you know what?

One of **their** very favorite people
in the **whole** world...
is

Great-Gramma Darling

because she's so sweet

and

beautiful

and

she loves to laugh,

but mostly
because...

She just loves them.

Epilogue

Dorothy Mary Raines was a waitress at the Sportsmen's Café in Mora, Minnesota, for 52 years until it closed in 2009 when she was 82 years old. We've been hoping that Gramma Darling would move up to Alaska to live with us. We would love to have her around, to enjoy her company, to hear her laughter, and to begin repaying her for a lifetime of unselfishly bringing happiness to others.

All of the events recorded here are actual memories. They left such vivid and lasting emotional impressions on my mind, truly an idyllic season of youth. She was my hero and will always be indescribably dear to me. I am thrilled to honor my darling grandmother by sharing this story with you.

Lissa Schroeder

For more information about the author, illustrator, and Gramma Darling herself, visit us online at www.grammadarling.com.

Gramma Darling's
Chocolaty Cherry Cake

Cake:

1 package of any chocolate cake mix

1 package instant chocolate pudding mix

1 can (21 oz) cherry fruit filling (It's richer with the larger can of cherries, if you like)

3 eggs

1/2 cup milk

Frosting:

1 cup sugar

5 Tbsp butter

1/3 cup milk

1 package (6 oz) semi-sweet chocolate chips

Preheat oven to 350 degrees. Lightly grease a 9 x 13 inch cake pan, or two 8 inch round pans for a layered cake. Combine the cake mix, chocolate pudding mix, cherry filling, eggs, and milk. Mix until well blended. Pour mixture into pan(s) and bake for 35-40 minutes, or until a toothpick inserted in the center comes out clean.

For frosting: In a small saucepan combine the sugar, butter, and milk. Bring to a low boil, stirring constantly, cook 1 minute. Remove from heat, stir in chocolate chips until melted and smooth. Spread over the cake when everything has cooled.

CPSIA information can be obtained at www.ICGtesting.com
Printed in the USA
BVIW12n1925080316
439539BV00004B/8